P9-DGZ-028

Tikal

AUTHOR'S NOTE

I'd like to extend special thanks to Dr. Christopher Jones, Senior Research Scholar, Retired, University of Pennsylvania
Museum, and author of *Understanding Maya Hieroglyphs; Excavations in the East Plaza of Tikal, Guatemala*; and
(with Linton Satterthwaite) *The Monuments and Inscriptions of Tikal*. He has been generous, wise and patient in making the
complex work of a lifetime of Tikal study accessible to the rest of us. (Any errors of fact or interpretation are mine alone.)
Thanks also to Tikal guide Antonio Ortiz, Jr., for parting the jungles of the Peten.
And thanks as always to the Writers Room for the room to read, reflect and write.

Other Books by Elizabeth Mann
The Brooklyn Bridge
The Great Pyramid
The Great Wall
The Roman Colosseum
The Panama Canal
Machu Picchu
Hoover Dam

Editor: Stuart Waldman
Design: Lesley Ehlers
Copyright © 2002 Mikaya Press
Illustrations Copyright 2002 © Tom McNeely

Cataloging-in-Publication Data available from the Library of Congress
ISBN 1-931414-05-X

PRINTED IN CHINA

Tikal

A WONDERS OF THE WORLD BOOK

BY ELIZABETH MANN
WITH ILLUSTRATIONS BY TOM MCNEELY

MIKAYA PRESS

NEW YORK

The only sounds were the splash of paddles dipping into the water and the trickle as they were lifted forward, the droplets leaving brief wing outlines alongside the wooden hull. The paddlers worked in silence, weary from the tropical heat and the exertion. Mute bundles and baskets lay in ponderous heaps at the bottom of the huge canoe. This was no villager's boat bearing a day's catch of fish. This was a trading canoe, one of many that glided swiftly on the rivers of Central America carrying goods of every sort from city to city.

The canoe had set out on the Motagua River nearly a month before laden with obsidian from mines near the city of Quirigua. The Yucatan Peninsula in the seventh century was a world without metals, so the black, glasslike rock was in great demand. Chips of obsidian had razor-sharp edges that were used for everything from sculpting limestone to piercing the flesh of enemies.

The paddlers guided the canoe down the Motagua to the Caribbean Sea and then traveled north along the coast. Turning inland again, they struggled against the current as they made their way up the Holmul River deeper into the jungles of the Peten. Eventually the jungle grew less dense. They saw more cleared fields and, occasionally, clusters of buildings.

Finally in the distance they could make out a tall pyramid towering over the landscape. They paddled faster at the sight, for it meant they were nearing their destination. The pyramid marked the heart of the great Maya city of Tikal.

Mexico

Yucatan
Peninsula

Mesoamerica

Gulf of Mexico

PETEN

Holmul River

• Calakmul

• Tikal

• Caracol

Caribbean Sea

• Dos Pilas

• Quirigua

Sierra de las Minas

Motagua River

• Copan

Pacific Ocean

The Maya had once lived along the Caribbean coast, but around 1200 B.C. they migrated inland to the Peten. It was a forbidding wilderness of rolling hills and tangled rain forest. Jaguars and poisonous snakes lay in wait for the unwary, and jungle plants were always ready to reclaim cleared farmland. Floods and droughts, heat and insects were part of the hard, dangerous life.

Still, the Maya survived. They hunted deer in the jungle, caught snails in the *bajos* (lowland swamps), and harvested wild plants. They built homes on high ground above the swamp waters and cleared fields by cutting trees in the jungle and burning them during the dry season. They planted maize (corn), beans, and squashes for a dependable food supply.

The Maya were a brilliant people, and against all odds, deep in the jungle, they developed a sophisticated civilization. They studied the world around them and learned about everything from astronomy and mathematics to farming and architecture. They developed a beautiful written language of glyphs (written symbols), which scribes used to capture their knowledge in books on pages made of tree bark. They measured the passage of days and years with remarkably precise calendars. Their religion was rich in exciting myths and powerful gods, and that richness was reflected in their paintings and stone carvings. The Maya thrived. Small villages grew to become grand cities with populations numbering in the tens of thousands.

There were nearly one hundred cities in the Peten, and they were alike in many ways. They shared a common religion, language, and knowledge. They were linked to each other through trade and through marriage. But each was unmistakably a separate kingdom, loyal to its own *ahau* (king), using its own style of art and architecture, and seeking its own wealth.

Tikal was settled in 800 B.C., later than the other cities, but it was one of the first to become large and wealthy. It was built on a limestone ridge that jutted up between two enormous *bajos*. Its location was the key to its great success.

Trade was the lifeblood of Mesoamerica. Luxuries–green jade from the Sierra de las Minas, exotic ceramic pots from Mexico, seashells and coral from the Caribbean–as well as humble necessities like salt and avocados moved constantly around the Yucatan. Whether they were destined for cities within the Peten or for more far-flung places in Mesoamerica, all goods traveled across the Yucatan by river. One network of rivers flowed east into the Caribbean Sea and another flowed west into the Gulf of Mexico, but there was no continuous river route that went all the way across the peninsula. To get from one river system to the other, traders had to unload the canoes and carry the goods on their backs through the jungle.

Tikal was in a unique position to take advantage of the overland part of the traders' journey. The city sat squarely on its ridge in the middle of one of the few passable overland routes between the east-flowing and west-flowing rivers. All goods being carried between the river systems had to pass through the city, and Tikal charged dearly for that privilege. That was the source of the city's wealth and power.

Tikal prospered and grew. New buildings, always grander than the ones they replaced, were raised upon the ruins of the old, and then they, too, were knocked down and built upon.

The center of Tikal was the highest part of the city. It was also the oldest, and it was crowded with palaces and pyramids. They were built of limestone blocks, and the walls were coated with limestone plaster. The walls were decorated with elaborate carvings and glyphs and then painted a brilliant shade of red.

The nobility lived in an area called the Central Acropolis in stone palaces with thick walls, narrow rooms, and high, peaked roofs. Soft skins of jaguars made the limestone beds considerably more comfortable, and servants made their lives easy.

Tikal was not as crowded beyond the city center, but it sprawled for miles in every direction. Clusters of houses sat atop smaller limestone hills that poked up from the *bajos*. Some, belonging to wealthy families, were made of limestone. Many more were made of thin wooden poles lashed together with vines and coated with plaster. Fronds from guano palms were used for the roof. They were not as sturdy as stone houses, but a new one could be built in just days.

The central courtyards were alive with the dogs, turkeys, and stingless honey bees that the Maya raised. Children raced around the cooking fires. Kneeling women rocked back and forth as they ground maize on *metates* (smooth stones) with *manos* (handheld grinding stones). Weavers passed shuttles back and forth across looms strung with bright cotton threads, creating beautifully patterned fabric. Palms, avocado trees, squashes, and peppers grew near the houses, and containers of beer fermented in *chultuns* (small chambers dug into the limestone bedrock). Beyond the houses were fields planted with maize.

All Maya buildings were set on solid platforms made of earth and stone. The platforms raised the buildings above the damp ground during the rainy season, and they served another important purpose as well. Family members were buried in tombs dug into the platforms. Each house became a memorial to the ancestors who once lived there. The platforms beneath these houses were small, but platforms for pyramids or palaces could be taller than a person's head and big enough to support several buildings.

As Tikal became wealthy and powerful, it was inevitable that it would draw the envy and resentment of its neighbors. Among the Maya, such resentment could lead to only one thing–war. Warfare was a way of life in the Peten. Cities, some barely a day's walk apart, often fought savagely with one another.

Sometimes they fought for wealth. Conquerors could profit handsomely by demanding payments, called tribute, from the defeated city. Sometimes they fought for religious reasons. Offering human blood to their gods was an important part of Maya religion. Enemies captured in battle were used for the sacrifices. If a noble was captured, so much the better. Their blood was more valuable to the gods.

Astronomers watched the skies and consulted their books. When the planet Venus was in the right position in the heavens, war began. Warriors in bright, feathered costumes attacked with spears, hatchets, and stone clubs. If a king was captured, the fighting ended abruptly, but wars sometimes lasted for years.

Warfare was such an important part of Maya life that even games took on a warlike seriousness, particularly their ball game. It was a rough sport played with a massive black rubber ball on a stone court. Players had to keep the ball in play without touching it with hands or feet. They wore thick padding to keep their ribs from being shattered by the heavy, fast-moving ball. The game was dangerous for ordinary players, but it was worse for enemy captives when they were forced to play as part of the ritual of sacrifice. Then the penalty for losing was beheading.

The Peten was rarely at peace, and alliances between cities were constantly shifting. Wars were fought. Friends became bitter enemies and new alliances were formed.

The cities of Caracol, Calakmul, and Dos Pilas, envious and probably a little frightened of their mighty neighbor, formed just such an alliance in the sixth century. In 562 Tikal suffered a humiliating defeat at their hands. Tikal's *ahau*, Double Bird, was captured, tortured, and sacrificed in Dos Pilas.

Humbled, Tikal was forced to make tribute payments of food, ceramics, and *cacao* beans to its conquering neighbors. Human tribute was demanded as well. Artists, scribes, craftspeople, and laborers from Tikal were forced to work in the enemy cities. Double Bird's son, Animal Skull, was allowed to become *ahau* of Tikal, but he was king in name only. In truth he was powerless.

The defeat marked the beginning of the darkest period in Tikal's long history. The marketplace grew quiet as trade was diverted to enemy cities. Tikal was impoverished. No grand palaces or pyramids were built during Animal Skull's reign, nor during the reigns of the three *ahaus* who came after him. Worst of all, these helpless kings were not allowed to perform the religious rituals and sacrifices that were so necessary to keep Tikal in harmony with its gods. For people who looked to hundreds of different gods for everything from plentiful rainfall to successful beekeeping, this must have been a cruel blow.

It wasn't until more than a century later that a leader would emerge who was strong enough to lead Tikal to its former greatness.

That leader was Hasaw Chan K'awil. He was the son of Shield Skull, the last of the four *ahaus* who had ruled Tikal during the time of darkness. Shield Skull was the only one of the four who had fought to free Tikal from its conquerors. His courage was great, but his efforts were not enough. He was captured following a battle in Dos Pilas and sacrificed, leaving Hasaw next in line for the throne.

Hasaw was a majestic figure, taller than his people by a head, and beautiful by Maya standards. Thanks to the boards that had pressed his head when he was an infant, his forehead was regally flattened. The small ball that had been hung inches in front of his tiny face had done its work, too. His eyes had focused on it and now were crossed fetchingly above his long, magnificently hooked nose. He wore his feathered ceremonial garments with the dignity and bearing of one who had been raised to rule.

Shield Skull had taught his son well. Displaying a wisdom beyond his years, Hasaw moved slowly and without fanfare as he took his father's place. He knew that he ruled only with the permission of Tikal's enemies. He proceeded cautiously, but he turned his every effort toward continuing his father's struggle to restore Tikal. Even the somber work of burying his beloved father became a part of that effort.

Portraits of kings were carved on large limestone blocks called *stelae*. Hasaw is shown on this one in an elaborate ceremonial garment and headdress. The glorious colors of the jade, coral, and feathers in his costume can only be imagined.

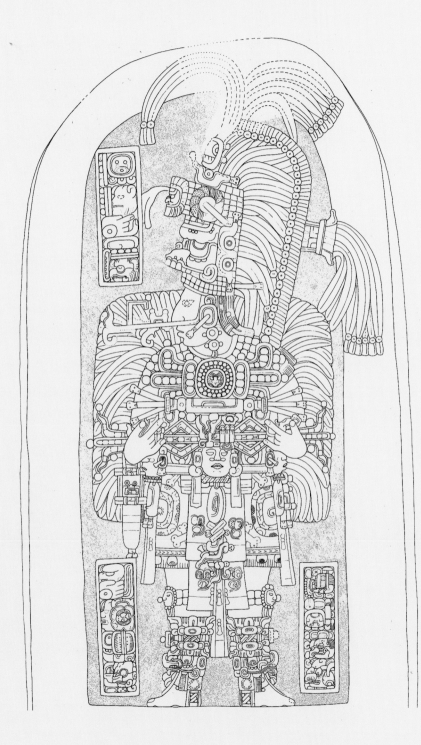

In the spring of 682, Hasaw Chan K'awil looked out over the crowds gathered in the Great Plaza from the steps of a newly completed pyramid. Deep within the solid stone was his father's tomb.

The pyramid was the first large-scale building project to be attempted in Tikal since 562. It was taller than anything that had ever been built before in Tikal or anywhere in the Peten. The temple at its top, reached by a single, dizzyingly steep staircase, appeared to float in the heavens. As Hasaw had intended, it was awe-inspiring, a fitting memorial to his great love for his father.

And as he had also intended, it was more than a memorial. In keeping with the Maya way of raising new structures upon the old, Hasaw built his father's pyramid temple on the ruins of the tomb of an earlier *ahau*, Stormy Sky. Nearly 250 years before, Stormy Sky had led Tikal in battle against an enemy invader from Mexico. The story of his victory had become an important Maya legend.

By carefully choosing where and how he built his father's pyramid, Hasaw sent a clear message to his people. Using the language of limestone, he told them that as *ahau* he would lead the city, just as Stormy Sky had, to victory and wealth. It was a message that must have been eagerly received in a city that had suffered for so long.

Hasaw's message was not one that Tikal's enemies wanted to hear. The rival cities were not eager to give up the tribute they had grown accustomed to, and they certainly didn't welcome Tikal as a trading rival. Hasaw had to speak to his enemies in another way. He chose the harsher language of blood.

As a grieving son Hasaw's first impulse must have been to strike at Dos Pilas and avenge his father's death. As a ruler he was too wise to rush into such an action. Vengeance may have tempted the young *ahau*, but he had to place the good of Tikal above his own desires. And so he waited and planned.

When the time was right to go to war, he didn't attack Dos Pilas. Instead, in a brilliant strategic move, he sent his soldiers to the north to attack the mightiest of all Tikal's enemies, Calakmul. Defeating Dos Pilas would have avenged his father's death, but only by defeating Calakmul could he destroy the enemy alliance forever.

It was not an easy victory. The bitter fighting went on for many years. At last, in 692, Calakmul was defeated and the alliance broke apart. The troubled times were over for Tikal. Free of its enemies after 130 years, the city could prosper once again.

The decorations painted on *cacao* cups are a colorful blend of glyphs and pictures.

The regal figures depicted on this cup stand proudly in elaborate feathered headdresses.

On this cup dancers leap in celebration, their ankle bells jingling, while the musician (left) pounds his drum and the kneeling figure (right) offers a cup of *cacao*.

Hasaw led Tikal to greatness that was unheard of even during the years of Stormy Sky. Giant trade canoes traveled the rivers, and the marketplace was again crowded and busy. Hasaw strengthened Tikal by forming alliances with other cities. He invited nobles and kings to Tikal and won them over with lavish feasts and dancing. He offered his guests chocolate beverages made of fermented *cacao* beans, an important gesture.

Cacao was so precious that the beans were used as a kind of money by the Maya. Offering it as a drink was an impressive way of showing off Tikal's wealth. The ceramic cups the *cacao* was served in were just as impressive. They were decorated with beautifully painted pictures and glyphs that proclaimed the glory of Tikal and its powerful *ahau*. Hasaw presented the cups to his guests as gifts. When they left, they took home with them a vivid reminder of all that was wonderful, and fearful, about Tikal and its great king.

And Hasaw continued to build, changing the face of the city with each new structure.

When Hasaw's wife, Lady Twelve Macaw, died, it was a painful loss for the young king. He built a remarkable pyramid to honor her memory. It was even taller and steeper than the one he had built for Shield Skull. He placed it in the Great Plaza, instead of in the crowded North Acropolis where royalty had always been buried. Lady Twelve Macaw's pyramid stood alone in that nearly empty sacred space, a unique and dramatic monument.

The temple that sat on top of Lady Twelve Macaw's pyramid was itself topped with a roofcomb, a high wall of limestone. Carved into the roofcomb was an enormous relief of Lady Twelve Macaw's face. Later, when Hasaw's own pyramid was built at the opposite end of the Great Plaza, his face was carved into the roofcomb of its temple also. As Hasaw had planned, he and his beloved queen could gaze at each other across the plaza for all eternity.

Just west of the North Acropolis, Hasaw built an unusual group of structures: a Twin Pyramid Group. It was not built to honor a person, but to honor time.

Time was sacred to the Maya. It was so important that they used two different calendars to mark the passing of every day and every year. The number twenty also had great significance. The Maya numbering system was based on twenty, instead of on ten as ours is. The end of a twenty-year period, a *katun,* was therefore an event of great importance, and it was greeted with elaborate festivities.

All Maya cities celebrated *katun* endings, but the building of Twin Pyramid Groups for the occasion happened only in Tikal. Hasaw's son and grandson continued the tradition after his death, building larger and larger Twin Pyramid Groups. In the end there were seven such groups in Tikal. The platform beneath the largest one covered nearly five acres!

Dancing and feasting were a part of the *katun*-ending celebrations, but there was a more serious side as well. Sacrifices were made to the gods, and the blood that was shed during these rituals was not always that of enemy captives.

Maya religious devotion was so strong that kings and queens, nobles, heads of ordinary families, men and women alike, willingly sacrificed their own blood to honor their gods. The bloodletting was not fatal, but it must have been very painful.

A Maya queen, for example, would pull a thorn-studded cord across her tongue until it bled. The queen allowed her blood to spill onto strips of bark paper in a ceramic bowl until she was too weak to continue. Then the blood-soaked paper was mixed with copal, a black, tarlike resin, and set on fire. As it burned, the aromatic smoke curled upward to the waiting gods.

Two very Maya important gods were the Hero Twins. Their story tells of the creation of the Maya world.

. . . . .

*I*n the Time of Darkness, before the world began, two gods, the twins Xbalanque and Huhnapu, were summoned to Xibalba, the underworld. They had been playing a ball game, and the noise had disturbed the underworld gods who slept beneath their ball court. The awakened Xibalba gods were furious, and their anger was no small matter. They had already slain the father and the uncle of the twins for disturbing their sleep with ball playing. It seemed that the twins were doomed to suffer the same fate.

The Xibalbans challenged the twins to play ball against them. They planned to kill them during the game. The twins accepted the challenge, but they had no intention of dying. They devised a crafty plan to outwit the underworld gods. During the game Huhnapu allowed himself to be killed; Xbalanque then brought him back to life.

The trick delighted and distracted the underworld gods. They forgot about punishing the Hero Twins and begged to be killed and brought back to life also. The twins were happy to oblige, but they only carried out the first part of the request. They never brought the gods back to life.

Once the underworld gods were destroyed, the Hero Twins rose up into the heavens. Huhnapu became the sun, Xbalanque became the moon, and together they shed light on the world. This ended the Time of Darkness and made the world safe for the creation of humans. From that time forth the Maya have told the story of the Hero Twins, who through their cunning and bravery, banished the darkness, brought light, and made it possible for people to exist.

. . . . .

Hasaw felt strongly connected to the myth of the Hero Twins. He saw a similarity between himself and the twin gods. He had used his wits and courage to end Tikal's years of enemy oppression, just as they had ended the Time of Darkness. He chose to build ceremonial ball courts to honor the two gods.

The Hero Twins appeared often on ceremonial *cacao* cups. Here Huhnapu (left) and Xbalanque are shown playing the ball game.

As remarkable as it was, Hasaw's reign was just the beginning of the most extraordinary century in Tikal's 1,500 year history. His son Yik'in Chan K'awil and his grandson Yax Ain II were also strong rulers. They continued to dominate other cities in battle. They captured prisoners and spilled their blood in sacrifices to the gods. They controlled trade in the Peten, increasing Tikal's wealth.

Like Hasaw, their most lasting marks were left in limestone. The Twin Pyramid Groups that they built for *katun* endings were all enormous projects, and there were others as well. Beginning with Hasaw's burial pyramid, which Yik'in built in the Great Plaza according to his father's wishes, they built a total of four gigantic single pyramids. The tallest one stood over twenty-one stories tall.

Although they built many ceremonial structures, the two *ahau*s didn't neglect the daily business of the city. Yik'in constructed a large, permanent marketplace east of the Great Plaza. He and Yax Ain II widened the raised causeways that led to it, paving them with plaster and building walls on both sides. The magnificent sweeping causeways provided visiting traders with a memorable entrance into Tikal. And, since the only entrance was through narrow, easily guarded gates, the causeways gave Tikal's rulers control over everything that came into the market.

Tikal covered more than twenty-five square miles of the Peten. What is shown here is only a part of the center of the city, less than one square mile.

1 The Great Plaza. Between 150 B.C. and 700 A.D. the entire two-and-one-half-acre plaza was covered with four different plaster floors. The most recent one was placed by Hasaw.

2 *Stelae.* Important people and events were captured in the glyphs and pictures carved on these large stone slabs. Tikal's rulers spoke to their subjects through the limestone *stelae*.

3 The North Acropolis, the royal burial area. Beneath the existing buildings lie the remains of a hundred earlier temples, tombs, pyramids.

4 Shield Skull's burial pyramid, built by his son, Hasaw.

5 Lady Twelve Macaw's burial pyramid, built by Hasaw.

6 Hasaw's burial pyramid, built by his son, Yik'in Chan K'awil.

7 Central Acropolis, where the palaces of royal and noble families were located.

8 Twin Pyramid Group, one of seven built by Hasaw and his descendants.

9 Twin Pyramid Group built by Yax Ain II in 790. It was the last of the seven, and the largest, with a platform that covered nearly five acres.

10 Pyramid built by Yax Ain II.

11 Plaster-lined reservoirs held a supply of water through the dry season.

12 Ceremonial ball court, built by Hasaw.

13 Marketplace, built by Yik'in Chan K'awil.

14 Causeway.

15 Homes.

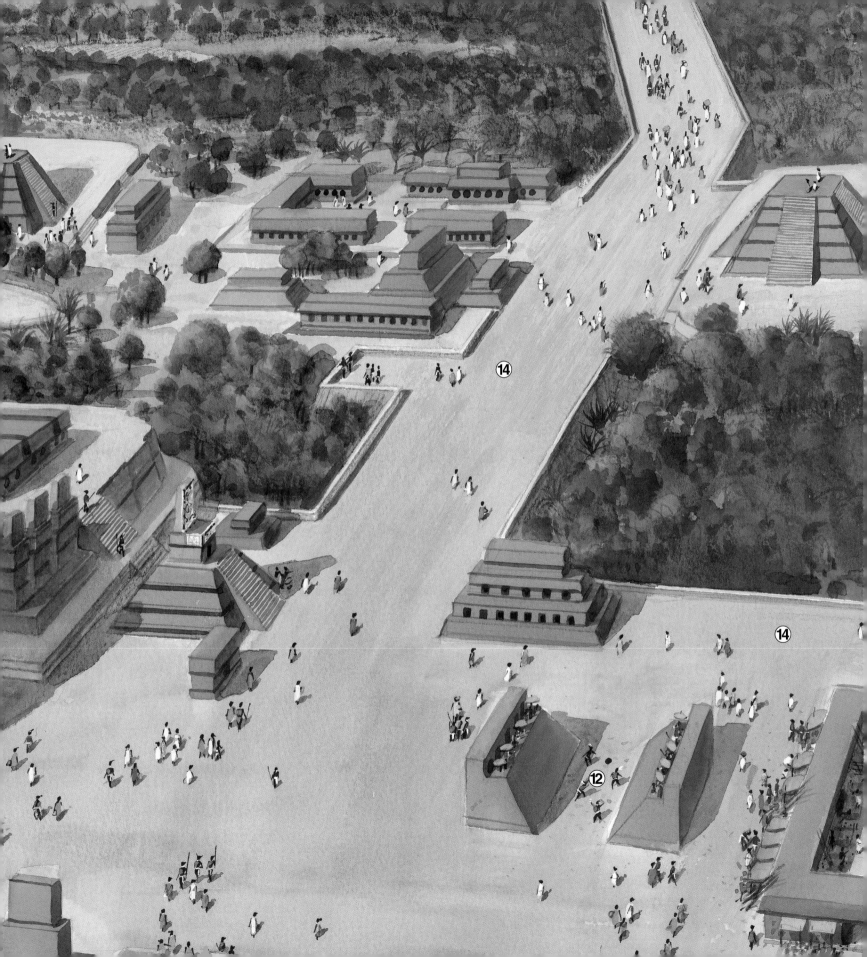

There seemed to be no end to the glory of Tikal during the reigns of these three great *ahaus*. The population was higher than it had ever been, construction was going on at an amazing pace, and Tikal was the most powerful city in the Peten.

And yet the glorious years did end, unexpectedly, completely, and mysteriously.

People died and others moved away. Trade stopped. Building stopped. The last *stela* was carved in 830. Kings, if there were any, left no traces in limestone to mark their passing. The city was abandoned, and the jungle swiftly reclaimed the silent fields and temples and markets. Barely one hundred years after the reign of Yax Ain II, Tikal had fallen into a time of darkness from which it would never recover.

The mystery of what happened in Tikal has intrigued archaeologists for a century and a half. Many fascinating theories have been suggested to explain why Tikal collapsed at the height of its wealth and power.

One theory suggests that hunger may have destroyed Tikal. The elaborate building projects of Hasaw and his descendants took many farmers out of their fields and put them to work on construction. The constant warfare took more farmers from their maize crops and sent them to attack neighboring cities. Builders and soldiers were not producing food, but they and their families still needed to eat. As strange as it may seem, it's possible that, in a time of apparent prosperity, there simply wasn't enough food for everyone.

Another theory suggests that a change in canoeing led to Tikal's end. For many centuries Maya canoes and their paddlers were no match for long trips on the open ocean. That was why the river routes across the peninsula were so important. It may have been that as boats and boating skills improved, travel by ocean became possible. If traders could move goods by sea all the way from Copan, say, to profitable markets in Mexico, they would have chosen to do so. There was no overland carrying, no jungle dangers, no relentless river currents. And if traders no longer passed through Tikal, the city's main source of wealth would have been lost.

Earthquake, drought, and disease are also possible reasons for the collapse, but no single theory or combination of theories has ever been proven.

And the mystery extends far beyond Tikal. It was not the only Maya city to be abandoned in the ninth century. Cities throughout the Peten, large and powerful, small and weak, suffered the same fate at the same time. They, too, grew silent and soon disappeared in the jungle growth. We still don't know what happened in the Peten a thousand years ago, and we may never know.

Many years later, in 1502, Christopher Columbus reported seeing large trading canoes in the waters off the Yucatan Peninsula. They were apparently the canoes of the Maya who had left the Peten centuries before and established cities on the northern Yucatan coast to take advantage of the new ocean trading routes.

Not long after, Spanish explorers arrived in the Yucatan looking for gold and for converts to Christianity. They found no gold, and the Maya were resistant to their religion, so they moved on. The diseases they carried with them lingered, and many Maya died. The cities on the Yucatan coast were soon abandoned just as those in the Peten had been.

It wasn't until the nineteenth century that the next European visitors arrived, drawn by rumors of lofty pyramids in the Peten. They slashed through the tangled jungle to find the ruins, and they marveled at the people who had built them. They couldn't read the glyphs on the *stelae* and *cacao* cups they found, so they relied on their imaginations to tell the story of the Maya.

They imagined a gentle people, led by scholarly priests, who moved softly through the perpetual rituals of worship and planting that defined their days. They imagined a people without kings, or warfare, or bloodshed, living contentedly in a peaceful world. This appealing picture of the Maya was accepted as truth for decades.

In the last fifty years, though, this story has been questioned. Beginning in the ruins of Tikal, scholars have been exploring Maya buildings, translating glyphs, and studying artwork. Thanks to their years of work, the Maya are no longer nameless, faceless jungle dwellers. They have become real people. We know about their wars, and about their legends. Great leaders, like Stormy Sky and Hasaw Chan K'awil and his descendants, have taken shape for us as complicated, real people who loved and celebrated, sacrificed and fought.

Following page. The Great Plaza and some of the surrounding structures as they appear today, including Hasaw's pyramid (left), Lady Twelve Macaw's pyramid (right), part of the North Acropolis (bottom left), and the Central Acropolis (top right).

TIMELINE

1200 B.C.*	Maya move inland to the Peten
800 B.C.*	Tikal first settled
456 A.D.	End of Stormy Sky's reign
562	Defeat of Tikal by Calakmul, Dos Pilas, and Caracol
679	Death of Shield Skull
682	Hasaw Chan K'awil takes the throne
682-695	Builds Shield Skull's pyramid
	Builds first Twin Pyramid Group
695	Tikal defeats Calakmul
695-734	Hasaw builds Lady Twelve Macaw's pyramid
	Builds ceremonial ball courts
	Builds second Twin Pyramid Group
734	Yik'in Chan K'awil takes the throne
734-768	Builds Hasaw's pyramid
	Builds marketplace
	Builds largest individual pyramid
768	Yax Ain II takes the throne
768-900	Builds causeway
	Builds two largest Twin Pyramid Groups
900*	Tikal abandoned

approximate dates

GLOSSARY

ahau– king

bajo– swampland

cacao– beans from which chocolate is made; used as money by Maya

causeway– an elevated roadway

chultun– a storage chamber dug into limestone bedrock

copal– hard resin taken from jungle trees and used as incense

glyph– a written symbol (an abbreviation of hieroglyphic)

maize– corn

mano– a handheld stone, usually granite, used to grind maize on a *metate*

metate– smooth stone upon which maize is ground with a *mano*

relief– image carved into a flat stone surface

stela (stelae plural**)**– large slab of limestone on which the Maya carved images and glyphs telling of important historic events

tribute– payment demanded of a defeated enemy

INDEX

CREDITS

Wilbur E. Garrett/ National Geographic Image Collection: *pp.* 44-45
Justin Kerr: *pp.* 24, 30, 33
University of Pennsylvania Museum (Negative # 69-5-55): *p.* 19

Works consulted in the preparation of this book
were written for adults. A bibliography is available
for interested teachers, librarians, and parents at:
www.mikaya.com

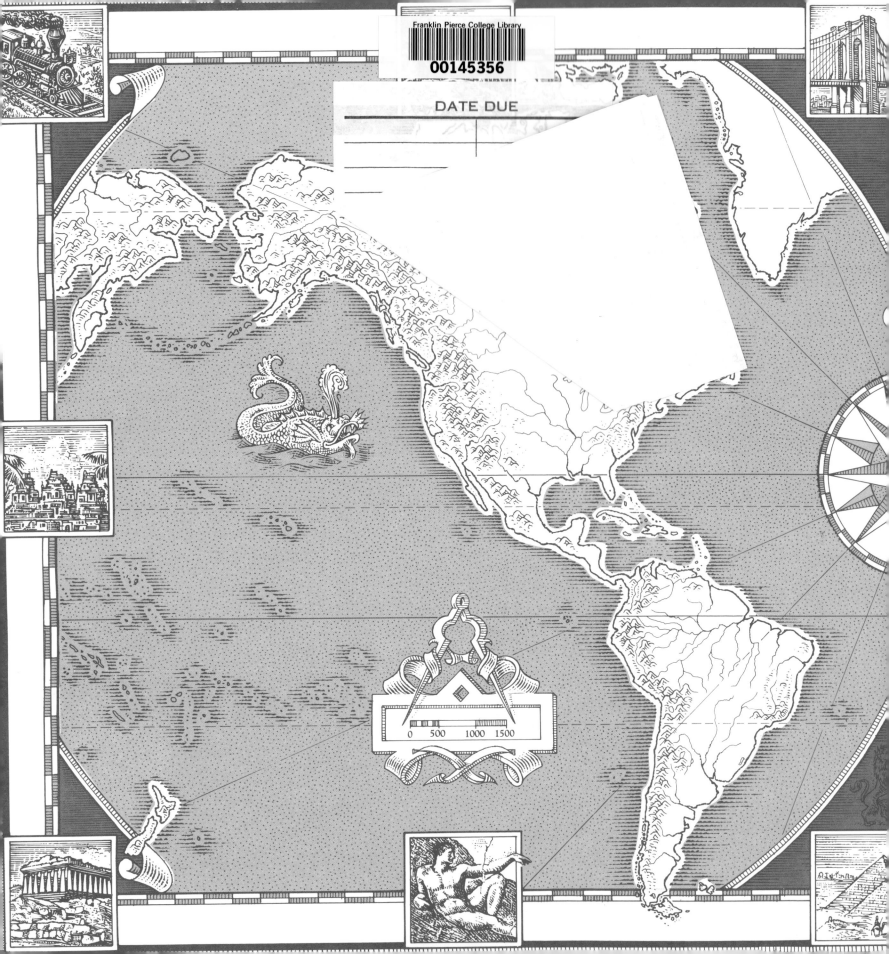

DATE DUE

0   500   1000   1500